Smart Agriculture

*How AI is Transforming Farming
and Food Production*

Table of Contents

1. Introduction 1

2. The Dawn of Smart Agriculture: An Overview 2

2.1. Understanding Smart Agriculture 2

2.2. Role of AI in Smart Agriculture 3

2.3. Internet of Things (IoT) and Precision Farming 3

2.4. Drones: A Game-Changer in Field Monitoring 4

2.5. Geo-Spatial Technologies for Site-Specific Crop Management 4

2.6. The Future of Smart Agriculture 4

3. Artificial Intelligence: A New Agricultural Revolution 6

3.1. The Evolution of AI in Agriculture 6

3.2. AI Technologies Transforming Agriculture 7

3.3. AI-fueled Precision Agriculture 7

3.4. AI and Sustainable Farming 8

3.5. Challenges in Implementing AI in Agriculture 9

3.6. AI: The Future of Agriculture 9

4. Decision Agriculture: Enhancing the Farmer's Intuition with AI . 11

4.1. How AI is Revolutionizing Decision Agriculture 11

4.2. Transformation of the Farming Landscape: AI in Practice . . . 12

4.3. Benefits and Challenges: The Road Ahead 13

5. The Digital Farmer: Technology in the Field 15

5.1. The Age of Autonomous Tractors and Robotics in Farming . . 15

5.2. Sensor-based Soil and Crop Monitoring 16

5.3. Precision Irrigation and Water Management 16

5.4. Predictive Analytics and Yield Optimization 17

5.5. The Power of Real-Time and Big Data in Farming 18

5.6. Farming Management Software: The Farmer's Virtual Companion 18

6. Sowing Seeds with Robots: Precision Agriculture and AI 20

   6.1. AI and Robotics: Pioneering Precision Planting 20

   6.2. Automated Soil Analysis and Seed Selection 21

   6.3. Navigating Unpredictability with Drones 22

   6.4. The Dawn of Robotic Weed Control 22

   6.5. The Big Picture: AI-powered Precision Agriculture 23

7. Weathering the Storm: Predictive Analytics and Climate

Resilience 24

   7.1. Building Climate Models for Predictive Analytics 24

   7.2. Predictive Analytics: Practical Applications 25

   7.3. Tools for Gathering Data 25

   7.4. Case Study: Predictive Analytics in Viticulture 26

   7.5. Future Scope: Climate Resilience and Smart Agriculture 26

8. From Drought to Bounty: AI in Irrigation and Water

Management 28

   8.1. The AI-Smart Irrigation Interface 28

   8.2. Water Management with AI and IoT 29

   8.3. Predictive Analytics for Optimal Irrigation 29

   8.4. Drones and AI-Assisted Irrigation 30

   8.5. The Future of AI in Irrigation 30

9. The Role of Big Data in Smarter Crop Management 32

   9.1. Understanding Big Data 32

   9.2. From Raw Data to Actionable Insights 33

   9.3. Big Data and Precision Agriculture 33

   9.4. Unleashing the Power of Remote Sensing 34

   9.5. IoT and Smart Farming 34

10. The Future Plate: How Smart Agriculture Impacts Food

Production 36

   10.1. Unveiling Smart Agriculture: An Overview 36

   10.2. Artificial Intelligence in Agriculture 36

10.3. The Automation Revolution 37

10.4. Vertical Farming and Hydroponics 37

10.5. AI and Genetically Modified Organisms (GMOs) 38

10.6. On the Plate: The Big Picture 38

11. The Road Ahead: Future Potential and Challenges for AI in Agriculture 40

11.1. The Promise of Precision Agriculture 40

11.2. Harnessing Big Data for Predictive Analytics 41

11.3. Automated Operations and Robotics 41

11.4. Integrating AI with Vertical Farming 42

11.5. Challenges on the Horizon 42

11.6. Conclusion 43

Chapter 1. Introduction

In this Special Report, we delve into the robust yet remarkably intricate world of Smart Agriculture, a rapidly evolving sector where artificial intelligence (AI) and farming converge. With down-to-earth evaluations, this report unpacks how AI's influence in agriculture is not only transforming the daily operations on a farm but also reshaping global food production. Whether you're a seasoned tech enthusiast, a farming professional, or a curious reader, this report blends technical depth with easy-to-understand insights. It's designed to weave you through the labyrinth of algorithms and drones, crop sensors, and predictive analytics, all the way to your dinner table. This isn't just about advances in technology; it's about the future of our sustenance. Prepare to embark on an enlightening journey that may just redefine your understanding of the farm-to-fork story.

Chapter 2. The Dawn of Smart Agriculture: An Overview

In the last few decades, agriculture has witnessed an extraordinary revolution. This transformation has been driven not just by the heavy machinery replacing human resources, but the sophistication and precision offered by advanced technologies such as Artificial Intelligence (AI) and Machine Learning (ML). This convergence of technology with farming has given birth to a new era of smart agriculture.

2.1. Understanding Smart Agriculture

Smart agriculture, also known as precision agriculture, embodies the integration of advanced technologies into existing farming practices to increase efficiency and productivity. This field converges numerous branches of technology such as AI, Internet of Things (IoT), Big Data, Robotics, and Geospatial technologies. Its essence resides in using these technologies to monitor a wide array of conditions - from crop conditions to weather patterns - at a high frequency and making data-driven decisions to optimize yields and manage resources.

Smart Agriculture is not just about integrating technology into farming. It necessitates a holistic understanding of the farm ecosystem and tailoring solutions, which are beneficial for both the farmers and the environment.

2.2. Role of AI in Smart Agriculture

The advent of AI in farming has been a game-changer. AI enables farmers to work smarter by automating tasks, analyzing vast data points in real-time, and making predictions about future conditions. It aids farmers in applying the right amount of pesticides and fertilizers, therefore improving crop health and reducing chemical runoff into local water sources.

Machine Learning (ML), a subset of AI, plays an instrumental role by allowing machines and software algorithms to improve automatically via the experience gained from mining a wide array of agricultural data sources. These encompass weather forecasts, past crop yields, soil properties, and more. AI-driven predictive modeling can predict crop productivity, pest infestations, and disease outbreaks - enabling farmers to manage operations proactively.

2.3. Internet of Things (IoT) and Precision Farming

IoT has been a key player in smart agriculture. It enables farm equipment and systems to communicate and share data with each other, creating an interconnected network that enhances automation and analytics capabilities. IoT devices - such as smart sensors for soil moisture, crop health, and GPS-enabled machinery - provide farmers with the critical real-time data they need to optimize and fine-tune their farming strategies.

GPS technology specifically is being deployed in equipment used for planting, fertilizing, and harvesting crops. These systems are capable of precise operations – reducing overlap, saving on input costs, and improving yield by ensuring a better distribution of resources.

2.4. Drones: A Game-Changer in Field Monitoring

Perhaps one of the most noticeable aspects of smart agriculture is the use of drones. Equipped with high-resolution cameras and various analysis tools, drones provide farmers with bird's-eye view images of their crops. This makes it possible to identify issues such as crop stress, disease, or pest infestations which otherwise might go unnoticed.

Moreover, drones can also be used for precise applications of pesticides and fertilizers - reducing exposure of harmful chemicals to humans and non-target areas.

2.5. Geo-Spatial Technologies for Site-Specific Crop Management

Satellite imagery and Geographic Information Systems (GIS) are also readily leveraged for more efficient crop management. These systems allow farmers to visualize their fields digitally, enabling them to observe any changes in crop color, height, and density. Precision farming using geo-spatial technologies enables the strategic use of inputs on a site-specific basis, helping to minimize waste and maximize yield.

2.6. The Future of Smart Agriculture

While smart agriculture is now a reality, the journey has just begun. The future of smart agriculture forecasts advancements in technologies such as vertical farming, precision gene editing, the Blockchain for traceability, and much more. As researchers and innovators continue to probe the potential of AI and other technologies, the intersection of farming technology is anticipated to blossom further.

This paradigm shift holds immense potential not just in achieving better yield and profitability for farmers, but also in resolving some of the most pressing global issues such as food security and climate change. Indeed, smart agriculture stands at the nexus of a triumphant trifecta - people, profit, and planet.

By diving into the intricate yet robust world of Smart Agriculture, we hope to have invoked a sense of the critical role technology is playing in shaping the future of farming - and in turn, global food production. AI's growing influence in agriculture is a testament to how the most traditional of our activities are being profoundly transformed by technology. Our farm-to-fork journey is being rewritten, and we are all fortunate enough to witness this unwinding narrative of innovation.

Chapter 3. Artificial Intelligence: A New Agricultural Revolution

Artificial intelligence (AI) has emerged as a remarkable revolution offering promising solutions to several challenges that traditional agricultural practices have encountered in recent years. With its roots deep in data analysis and machine learning techniques, AI has been progressively deployed across agricultural operations for improved productivity, risk mitigation, and sustainability.

3.1. The Evolution of AI in Agriculture

AI in agriculture isn't a modern invention; its origins dated back several decades when tech experts started experimenting with early forms of computational intelligence for crop management. The advancements in technology, along with a growing need to enhance crop yield and optimize resource use, set the stage for the integration of AI in the agricultural sector.

The global food demand is anticipated to increase by 60% by 2050 due to an exponential rise in the world's population. This demand, coupled with the detrimental effects of climate change, has put immense pressure on the agricultural sector. The advent and propulsion of AI in this space is expected to help meet these soaring demands and combat the agricultural challenges related to climate change and natural resources limitations.

3.2. AI Technologies Transforming Agriculture

AI technologies - machine learning, computer vision, predictive analytics, and IoT, among others - are changing the face of agriculture. They provide real-time data and insights to farmers, enabling them to make quicker and more informed decisions. Below are some of the prominent AI technologies that are leading the agricultural revolution:

- **Machine Learning:** Machine learning (ML) aids in creating more sophisticated models of existing farming techniques. It enables the anticipation of potential problems and provides actionable insights to make informed decisions. It plays an integral part in predictive analytics, which will be discussed later.

- **Computer Vision:** Drones equipped with computer vision can scan whole fields more rapidly and accurately than humans, detecting pests, analyzing soil conditions, and gauging plant health.

- **Predictive Analytics:** Predictive analytics involves using ML algorithms to predict future outcomes based on historical and current data. It can predict weather impacts, disease outbreaks, and crop yields - instrumental in crop risk management.

- **Internet of Things (IoT):** IoT devices like smart sensors for soil moisture and nutrients, GPS-guided automated machinery, and real-time weather monitoring systems are crucial in modern farming.

3.3. AI-fueled Precision Agriculture

Precision agriculture stands as one of the most tangible applications of AI. It is an approach to farm management that uses AI and IoT to optimize field operations. It pivots on the principle that each part of a field possesses unique characteristics which, when accurately measured and evaluated, can lead to improved total farm production. This reduces cost and environmental impact by minimizing unnecessary application of inputs, such as water and fertilizer.

Through precision agriculture, farmers can gather real-time data about their crops and fields. By leveraging information like soil composition, moisture levels, weather data, and pest infestation, farmers can target specific areas rather than uniformly applying treatments across entire fields.

GPS technology allows farmers to map their fields accurately, while various sensors monitor the soil and crops, transmitting this data back for further analysis. Machine learning models can then process this vast amount of data, predicting patterns and offering actionable insights that drive decision-making and operational changes.

3.4. AI and Sustainable Farming

AI can play a significant role in promoting sustainable farming methods. By optimizing inputs like water and fertilizer usage, precision farming paves the way for more sustainable practices. Remote sensing technologies, predictive analytics, and machine learning can provide early warnings about pest outbreaks or disease, allowing farmers to apply pesticides and other treatments only when necessary.

Further, AI can enable more nuanced climate change modeling, providing predictions about shifts in weather patterns and the likely impacts on crop production. This assists farmers in planning their planting and harvesting schedules more efficiently, reducing waste and boosting yields.

AI's potential extends to reducing post-harvest losses through smart storage systems that utilize sensors to monitor temperature, humidity, and spoiling gas levels. In doing so, AI technology can extend the shelf life of the produce, ensuring minimal waste and maximum utilization of the harvest.

3.5. Challenges in Implementing AI in Agriculture

Although AI has immense potential in agriculture, it's essential to address certain challenges posed by the amalgamation of these two intricate fields. Infrastructure limitations, particularly in developing regions, remain a significant hurdle. Despite the benefits of AI technologies, the lack of necessary hardware, like sensors and drones, as well as software, including reliable internet connectivity, hampers their adoption.

Moreover, the cost of implementing AI technologies can be onerous, especially for smallholder farmers. Coupled with a lack of training or understanding of these technologies, this lack of affordable access poses a further barrier to entry for many farmers.

Finally, ethical and privacy implications need consideration. Data collection is an integral part of AI-powered technologies. Ensuring that this information is secure and used ethically will be vital as AI's role in agriculture continues to expand.

3.6. AI: The Future of Agriculture

Despite the prevalent challenges, the overarching consensus hints at the invaluable role AI is set to play in the future of the agricultural sector. While we're witnessing the dawn of AI's impact on farming, it's only the beginning. Going forward, we're likely to see more sophisticated predictive analytics, further integration of IoT devices, and relentless efforts to make AI more accessible to farmers of all sizes.

The dawn of AI's influence on farming brings the hope to balance increasing food demand against the imperative to reduce environmental impact, ensure the efficient utilization of resources, and maintain agricultural profitability. As researchers continue to harness the power of AI, the sector may ultimately witness what could indeed be termed a new agricultural revolution.

Chapter 4. Decision Agriculture: Enhancing the Farmer's Intuition with AI

Decision agriculture is not a new concept. Since time immemorial, farmers have used their intuition, honed by years of experience, to make critical decisions: when to sow, what crop to plant, how to protect their harvest from pests and diseases, and when to harvest. They've relied on local knowledge, heritage wisdom, trial-and-error, and plain gut feelings. However, today's vast technology's advance, particularly Artificial Intelligence (AI), offers tools that can augment and enhance that instinctive know-how, turning intuition into data-driven decision making. AI doesn't replace the farmers; it empowers them.

4.1. How AI is Revolutionizing Decision Agriculture

AI technologies use algorithms and machine learning for predictive analysis that can optimize farming operations. IoT devices gather data from soil sensors, weather stations, drones, and satellite imagery, creating a vast and intricate data web. Through the AI lens, this data becomes meaningful and operational, allowing farmers to make precise, informed decisions that maximize productivity and sustainability. The power of AI lays in its ability to convert vast amounts of information into actionable insights about plant health, soil status, weather patterns, pest infestations, and yield predictions.

Deep learning models, a branch of AI, are particularly suited for analyzing these complex data stacks. They can recognize patterns and learn from information, eventually developing predictive capabilities. For instance, a model can learn to predict disease outbreaks based on plant color patterns or anticipate rain based on a sequence of past weather patterns.

AI can also bring precision to the allocation of resources like water, fertilizers, and pesticides. By monitoring soil and crop conditions in real-time, AI enables precision farming techniques that use analytics to adjust resource levels to each plant's needs. This not only leads to increased yield but also promotes sustainability by reducing the usage of resources.

4.2. Transformation of the Farming Landscape: AI in Practice

Imagine a day in the life of a farmer equipped with AI tools. Let's call him John. His day starts with a digest of reports generated overnight by various sensors and devices deployed on his farm. Deep learning algorithms analyze this data, predicting the weather for the day, showcasing soil hydration levels and nutrient status, assessing plant growth and health, and even warning of possible pest or disease invasions. As John makes his morning rounds, he is armed with incredibly precise insights, guiding his decisions throughout the day.

John's tractor is no ordinary piece of machinery now. It is equipped with GPS tracking, IoT devices and AI algorithms making it a cornerstone of his smart farming operations. As it moves across the fields, it measures soil composition and moisture levels, adjusting water and fertilizers distribution accordingly. This tractor even optimizes its route to reduce fuel consumption and soil compaction.

One of John's most significant worries is pest infestation and disease outbreaks. AI comes to the rescue with sophisticated image recognition techniques that spot telling changes in plant coloration or leaf pattern. Drone-mounted cameras sweep over the farm, capturing images that are later analyzed by deep learning models. John gets alerts on his smartphone at the first sign of trouble.

Predictive analytics are John's crystal ball when it comes to yield estimation. By extrapolating climate data, nutrient availability, disease occurrences, and growth trajectories, AI algorithms provide him with an estimate of the volumes he'll be hauling to the market, well before the harvest begins.

4.3. Benefits and Challenges: The Road Ahead

Despite its potential, AI in agriculture is still maturing. While the benefits are apparent, various challenges need addressing.

From an adoption perspective, technology literacy and connectivity are significant hurdles. Not all farmers are tech-savvy like John, and not all farms have the infrastructure necessary for deploying AI technologies. Furthermore, AI algorithms require large datasets to deliver accurate predictions, and data collection remains a challenge in many parts of the world.

On the practical side, AI models' efficacy can vary by crop type, geographical location, and local climate conditions. It means the algorithms need continual adjustment and fine-tuning, demanding continuous data flows, and complex support structures.

On the positive side, governments and businesses are recognizing these challenges and investing in solutions. Policymakers are revising regulations to encourage technology adoption, and corporations are investing in startups developing innovative solutions.

As AI continues to evolve, it will undoubtedly redefine decision agriculture. We can expect even wider impacts, from crop identification and protection against new pests and diseases to optimization of supply chains and market predictions. In the not-so-distant future, every farmer will have access to tools that enhance their intuition with AI, opening a new chapter in the story of agriculture.

Chapter 5. The Digital Farmer: Technology in the Field

As dawn breaks, the modern farmer awakens not just to the crowing of the roosters or the morning chorus of songbirds, but also to an orchestra of digital notifications. They know their fields intimately, yet rely on complex algorithms, rather than experience alone, to understand the subtleties in their land. Each day the task is the same - feed the world, but the playbook has dramatically changed. From tractors that drive themselves to drones that monitor crop health, from sensor-enabled irrigation systems to innovative yield predictions machines, the distillation of farming into a series of data points is the reality of today's Digital Farmer.

5.1. The Age of Autonomous Tractors and Robotics in Farming

Remember the image of a dedicated farmer driving a tractor across his or her broadacre? That's a fading archive in the annals of agricultural history. The tractor is still here, but the farmer may be somewhere else entirely - perhaps even behind a computer - handling several such autonomous machines simultaneously.

Farmbots, small robots designed for scale, plant seeds with exact precision, take care of weeding and administer fertilizers selectively. Drones hover relentlessly over the fields scanning, identifying threats, cataloguing data, and building invaluable aerial portraits of the farm. They don't replace farmers; rather, they infuse them with superhuman abilities - the power to be everywhere and see everything more clearly.

These are machines tirelessly adhering to a methodical routine, devoid of human sundry parameters like boredom, fatigue or dinner-time. This technical revolution sprung from the intersection of AI, machine learning, and robotics making autonomous farming not just a specter of the future but also of the present.

5.2. Sensor-based Soil and Crop Monitoring

Just as a doctor might use a thermometer or blood test to understand a patient's wellbeing, a digital farmer uses an array of sensor technology to comprehend the health of their soil and crops. Sensors buried in the fields monitor soil moisture, nutrients, and pH levels. These data points, the pulse of the farm, can trigger smart irrigation systems, automatically ensuring plants receive the right amount of water and nutrients based on real-time conditions.

Optical sensor technologies are also changing farmers' understanding of their crops. Multispectral analysis helps determine crop health more precisely, highlighting distressed or diseased areas invisible to the human eye before any notable damage occurs.

On the horizon looms the promise of nanosensors, infinitesimal devices that could dwell within a crop's physiology, transmitting updates related to growth, water stress, absorption of nutrients, and more. The scope seems immense if we heed Moore's law and its bearing on sensor tech.

5.3. Precision Irrigation and Water Management

The concept of precision irrigation might seem paradoxical to the image of sprinklers indiscriminately drenching a field. Precision irrigation is about applying water and fertilizers judiciously, based on the distinct requirements of different areas within the same field. Precision here isn't just metric; it is an ethos, a testament to responsible farming.

By linking sensor data with responsive watering systems, a digital farmer ensures that irrigation is reactive to the farm's minute-to-minute needs. Smart irrigation is about giving what's needed, where it's needed and just as importantly, when it's needed. This practice doesn't just reduce water waste and preserve vital resources, it also optimizes yield and promotes healthier crop growth.

5.4. Predictive Analytics and Yield Optimization

Farmers have always had to think ahead to predict weather patterns or pest invasions. Now, advanced predictive algorithms deliver proactive solutions rather than reactive firefighting. Accumulated data feeds sophisticated models that can predict yield, disease outbreaks, or pest attacks far more accurately than intuition or experience.

Crop-yield prediction, using predictive analytics, aids farmers in planning the planting schedule, managing resources, and optimizing output. In doing so, the approach minimizes uncertainty and maximizes productivity.

Mitigating threats from disease or pest is another challenge. Predictive analytics allow for proactive responses ensuring farmers combat these problems even before they arise. The efficacy of such preemptive strikes is an example of the technology augmenting age-old wisdom.

5.5. The Power of Real-Time and Big Data in Farming

Every moment counts in a farm's life-cycle. Real-time data doesn't allow market conditions, disease signs or weather anomalies to go unnoticed or unattended. Alerts can trigger automatic adjustments in the machinery. Every bit of data is essential, and the term 'irrelevant information' is becoming redundant in high-tech agriculture.

Big Data, the collective information farm operations generate, is analyzed and applied to create systems that are responsive, resilient, and adaptive. The beauty of this seemingly abstract ocean of information is that it boils down to one of the toughest tangible tasks - producing food.

However, navigating this data deluge requires capable analytical tools and, often, the ability to make complex decisions based on comprehensive data analysis. This need opens the path for more sophisticated farming management software, which we will explore next.

5.6. Farming Management Software: The Farmer's Virtual Companion

Farming management software serves as the linchpin tying together various digital farming aspects - a cornerstone of data management and decision-making in modern farming. This software can handle tasks from sowing to harvesting, aggregating sensor readings, drones' aerial data, market trend updates, and more.

Well beyond mere data collection, these tools facilitate smart farming decisions based on comprehensive real-time data analysis. They're the digital farmer's most accessible interface with intricate AI technology, a commander's console where operations are directed and future strategies planned.

Conscious agriculture is no new phenomenon. However, infusing it with AI has led to precision unimaginable until the recent past. The powerful trifecta of data, technology, and complexity narrates the story of the Digital Farmer. This is not just a tale of progress and profits, but one of how we confront global challenges of food production and the environment.

Chapter 6. Sowing Seeds with Robots: Precision Agriculture and AI

Gone are the days when a farmer's day started and ended with daylight. Today, robotic technologies are penetrating the agricultural industry, melding with time-honored practices to propel the sector into the future.

Farming has always been an intricate balance of art and science, honed through generations of farmers adapting to ever-changing weather, pests, and market conditions. However, in recent years, the emergence of precision agriculture — a farming management concept leveraging observed, measured, and responded variables to optimize returns on inputs while preserving resources — is shifting the dynamics of traditional farming.

Coupled with artificial intelligence and robotics, precision agriculture is revolutionizing the way farmers sow, nurture, and harvest crops. Let's explore this transformative shift in greater detail.

6.1. AI and Robotics: Pioneering Precision Planting

One of the inaugural steps in the farming calendar is sowing the seeds. Precision is key in seed placement for optimized yield, and this is precisely where AI and robotics come in handy. These technologies have ushered in a new era of 'precision planting', where every seed's location is controlled to an incredible degree.

AGCO's Fendt Momentum, an AI-based high-tech planter, for example, makes the process of seed placement more accurate and uniform. Controlled by AI algorithms, the planter can sense and adapt to topographic and soil variations across the field. This allows it to place seeds at the ideal depth and spacing to ensure each plant gets enough nutrients for optimal growth.

Moreover, AI technologies enable intelligent monitoring of planting processes in real-time, with anomalies being flagged for immediate rectification. This precision planting increases the likelihood of seed germination, reduces input costs, and promises higher crop yields.

6.2. Automated Soil Analysis and Seed Selection

AI and robotics do more than merely plant seeds—they can also analyze the soil's properties and select the right seeds to plant. These robots use sensors to measure variables like soil pH, moisture, and nutrient content, feeding this data into AI algorithms that derive actionable insights.

Take Small Robot Company, an UK-based agtech firm that utilizes AI-powered robots called Tom, Dick, and Harry. Tom uses AI and machine learning to analyze soil and crop health. Based on this analysis, Dick micro-sprays exact quantities of fertilizers, pesticides or fungicides, while Harry completes precision drilling, dispensing exactly what seeds are needed where.

The adoption of AI in automated soil analysis and seed selection can result in tailored and environmentally friendly farming. Each crop receives the nutrients it needs, reducing fertilizer overuse, and enhancing soil health while mitigating environmental damage.

6.3. Navigating Unpredictability with Drones

Farming is an inherently unpredictable venture. Drones, equipped with AI, are revolutionizing how farmers deal with this unpredictability. Capable of scanning fields quickly and accurately, drones provide farmers with a bird's-eye view of their crops—something traditional human scouting could never offer.

Drones equipped with multispectral imaging cameras can capture data invisible to the naked eye. By identifying plant stress or disease early on, they give farmers the chance to react quickly, saving crops in the nick of time.

Moreover, smart drones can be programmed to follow specific routes and conduct regular surveillance. They collate data over time and provide AI-powered predictive analysis, helping farmers anticipate issues before they arise.

6.4. The Dawn of Robotic Weed Control

Weeds are a farmer's nightmare, causing substantial losses in yields. AI and robotics are now stepping in to help manage this pervasive problem. Robotic weed controllers like Blue River Technology's See & Spray use AI to identify and pinpoint the location of weeds in a field.

These smart machines use an arsenal of cameras to capture a variety of images, which are then processed by deep learning algorithms. They differentiate between crops and weeds, spraying herbicides only on the latter, minimizing chemical input. This level of precision is not only beneficial for crop health, but it's also a significant stride towards environmentally friendly farming.

6.5. The Big Picture: AI-powered Precision Agriculture

The intersection of AI and robotics in precision agriculture isn't just about increasing productivity—it's about sustainability and resilience. From sowing seeds with pinpoint accuracy, analyzing soil quality, controlling weed growth, to predicting crop health, these technologies are creating a new class of smart farms.

As the world's population snowballs, and climate change brings about unpredictable weather patterns, these technologies will be vital in maintaining and improving global food security. Yet, as with all transformative technologies, there are challenges and potential pitfalls.

There may be issues of adoption, particularly among smallholder farmers who may lack the resources or know-how to integrate these technologies. There are also privacy concerns, regulatory hurdles, and job displacement worries. However, perhaps the most critical question of all, one that may shape agriculture's future, is whether these technologies can be used equitably, ensuring all participants in the global food chain benefit.

Ultimately, as we delve deeper into the era of smart agriculture, powered by AI and robotics, the goal should not be technology for technology's sake. Instead, it should be about harnessing these innovations to nurture a future where food production is sustainable, resilient, and inclusive, where technology enhances human labor rather than replacing it, and where the land used is respected for its intrinsic value. In other words, a future where agriculture is truly 'smart'.

Chapter 7. Weathering the Storm: Predictive Analytics and Climate Resilience

The impacts of global climate change loom large over agriculture's horizon, yet emerging technologies offer a beacon of hope. Through the implementation of predictive analytics, farmers worldwide are finding ways to weather the literal and figurative storms, utilizing cutting-edge data strategies to anticipate climatic variations and adjust their strategies accordingly.

7.1. Building Climate Models for Predictive Analytics

Key to predictive analytics in agriculture is the construction of accurate, reliable climate models. These models, created using a combination of historical weather data, current weather observations, and advanced mathematical algorithms, are capable of predicting future weather patterns with an astonishing degree of accuracy. Unlike the rudimentary equipment of days gone by, modern sensors can monitor a wide range of meteorological conditions - from temperature and precipitation, to UV radiation, soil moisture, and wind speed.

But climate models aren't confined to the realm of meteorological data alone; they also incorporate a variety of additional factors that may impact agricultural productivity. These can include data from topographical surveys, information about local flora and fauna, and even sociological data such as population growth or economic trends. The result is a highly precise, multifaceted model of climate behavior that is tailored for agricultural needs.

7.2. Predictive Analytics: Practical Applications

Simply put, predictive analytics enables farmers to forecast future events based on available data. This includes scheduling planting and harvest times for maximum yield, preparing for or even preventing disease infestations, and managing water usage – all with an eye towards the projected weather patterns. This level of precision is critical in the face of climate change, as previously predictable seasonal patterns become increasingly erratic.

Studies show that implementing predictive analytics can lead to a 10-20% increase in crop yield, a substantial gain for both small-scale farmers and larger agricultural operations alike. For example, by following the disease prediction models, a farmer can take preventive measures in advance, ensuring the crops are shielded from any impending outbreak. Similarly, predictive models of rain patterns and temperature ranges can aid in deciding the best planting times and crop variety for a given season.

7.3. Tools for Gathering Data

While climate models and predictive analytics are promising strategies in mitigating the impacts of climate change, their efficacy relies on the quality of data gathered. Here, technological advances in remote sensing and IoT (Internet of Things) provide the underpinnings for data collection.

Satellites and remote sensing drones provide valuable data around weather conditions, pest infestation, and crop health. Portable weather stations and handheld devices accumulate real-time field data, and IoT devices like soil sensors and weather stations placed around the farm capture microclimate conditions.

These tools are networked together, enabling real-time data sharing and analysis. This resource provides farmers state-of-art prediction models which are updated in real-time for operational efficiency.

7.4. Case Study: Predictive Analytics in Viticulture

An interesting application of predictive analytics arises in viticulture or the science of grape production. Vineyards, highly susceptible to minute changes in climate, have greatly benefited from predictive analytics. A variety of tools and methodologies have been developed specifically for this field.

One such tool is the Grape Remote-sensing Atmospheric Profile and Evapotranspiration eXperiment (GRAPEX), which provides high-resolution weather forecasts and evapotranspiration models for vineyards. From predicting the onset of damaging weather conditions like frost and heatwaves to scheduling irrigation systems based on soil and weather data, this tool has proven indispensable for grape growers. The evidence lies in the improvement of grape quality and yield, sustainable water management, and reduced operational costs.

7.5. Future Scope: Climate Resilience and Smart Agriculture

The future of predictive analytics in agriculture is propelled not only by technology but also by the increasing demand for climate resilience. As weather patterns continue to shift under the impact of climate change, it is clear that predictive analytics will continue to play a critical role in both small-scale and industrial farming operations.

Advancements are likely to occur in new areas too. For example, the incorporation of AI and machine learning to make climate models and predictions more accurate is an exciting development. The ultimate goal: aligning the farming community and technologists towards maximizing both productivity and sustainability.

In closing, as we rally against the challenges of climate change, predictive analytics offers an efficient tool to minimize its impacts on agriculture. This gives farmers a new level of knowledge and foresight, enabling them to react timely and effectively to the capriciousness of weather, ensuring the sustenance of the population. Indeed, the marriage of AI and agriculture signifies a new dawn in managing climate resilience.

Chapter 8. From Drought to Bounty: AI in Irrigation and Water Management

Water scarcity, especially with burgeoning populations and climate change, is one of the most acute problems the world faces today. However, contemporary breakthroughs in AI and related technologies promise a path to more efficient and sustainable use of water resources. Artificial intelligence unfolds an array of exciting possibilities, playing a pivotal role in precision irrigation and water management systems, thus turning arid farms into bountiful fields.

8.1. The AI-Smart Irrigation Interface

Farming's traditional element, irrigation, is ushering into an era of precision and efficiency, revolutionized by AI. Smart irrigation systems powered by AI algorithms are reducing water wastage and maximizing crop yield. The first-generation smart sprinklers were connected to weather forecasts; however, the latest generation leverages AI, which combines historical weather data, current soil conditions, and the crop's individual hydration requirements.

These AI-equipped devices also adapt to real-time variations in the weather, making necessary adjustments, and deliver the right amount of water to the crops at the right time. For instance, the system can dial down water supply during about-to-start rainfall, harnessing natural resources and preventing waterlogging in fields. When pervasive technologies like big data analytics, machine learning (ML), and Internet of Things (IoT) coincide with AI, there's a substantial improvement in crop irrigation and water management.

8.2. Water Management with AI and IoT

The amalgamation of AI and IoT is pivotal for smart water management. IoT devices, stationed across the farm, constantly gather data about environmental factors such as temperature, humidity, rainfall, wind speed, and soil conditions. This colossal dataset is then subjected to AI algorithms which, while analyzing the data, offer actionable insights that farmers can harness.

For example, sensor-based systems can detect moisture levels in the soil, whereby an AI algorithm analyzes patterns from past years and uses predictive analytics to suggest optimum watering schedules. Farmers can remotely monitor and control the irrigation systems, thereby reducing water use, saving costs, and increasing productivity.

Another application is the use of IoT in monitoring water usage and detecting leaks in irrigation systems. Real-time data from wired equipment allows early leak detection, wherein AI aids in determining the leak's location and severity, ensuring rapid rectifying actions.

8.3. Predictive Analytics for Optimal Irrigation

AI's breathtaking ability to analyze and predict is a game-changer for the agricultural industry. Predictive analytics tools, using complex AI algorithms, process large volumes of data and make precise predictions about future events, including the weather and crop health.

Moreover, predictive analytics isn't limited to managing water resources. It helps determine which crops to plant based on rainfall forecasts and soil conditions. Therefore, farmers are able to plan better, optimize the watering system, and maintain healthier crops, leading to better agricultural yield.

Even though these analytics tools are highly sophisticated, user-friendly interfaces and data visualization ensure that they are accessible to farmers and agricultural professionals lacking in computer know-how.

8.4. Drones and AI-Assisted Irrigation

Unmanned aerial vehicles, commonly known as drones, are becoming indispensable in modern agriculture. Paired with AI, these drones provide insights about water distribution and crop health by collecting high-resolution images of the farmland. Besides, they can also identify areas of over or under-irrigation, enabling farmers to address specific needs of different zones within a farm, promoting sustainable water use.

Through intelligent image recognition technology, AI algorithms can identify signs of water stress or diseases in crops before they become visible to the human eye. Early detection increases the chances of survival for unhealthy crops and aids in preventing disease from spreading to the surrounding vegetation.

8.5. The Future of AI in Irrigation

As we glimpse into the future of AI-powered irrigation, automated farms and intelligent water distribution systems can be envisioned. As technology evolves, AI will likely facilitate the creation of virtual crop models to simulate water consumption patterns and nutrient requirements under various conditions. These models can predict irrigation needs with higher accuracy, leading to even more efficient use of water.

In conclusion, AI-powered systems hold massive potential for improving irrigation strategies and refining water management, which can revolutionize the agricultural sector. Investments in these technologies are not mere enhancements, but rather, they're vital contributions to the future of sustainable farming and a steadfast attempt at dealing with climate change. The advent of AI in irrigation marks the beginning of a journey that leads from drought to bounty.

Chapter 9. The Role of Big Data in Smarter Crop Management

In the realm of artificial intelligence's application in agriculture, one ubiquitous factor that plays a mighty role is Big Data. The advent and propagation of sensor technologies, satellite imagery, and geographic information systems curate a slew of information that provides an all-encompassing view of a farming system. Careful interpretation of this data fuels smarter crop management strategies, ultimately refining the efficiency, productivity, and sustainability of our agricultural framework.

9.1. Understanding Big Data

In the simplest terms, Big Data denotes extensive sets of information that exceed traditional computing capacities. In the agricultural domain, these data streams derive from several sources — weather patterns, soil properties, crop health details, pest/fungus occurrences, and more — and their analysis helps drive better-informed decisions and actions.

Critical to making sense of this broad array of information is data analytics. This process typically involves data collection, cleansing, management, and ultimately analysis, to reveal and interpret patterns, trends, and associations relevant to farming practices. With the increasing prevalence of precision agriculture, the importance of big data analytics in crop management is becoming more apparent.

9.2. From Raw Data to Actionable Insights

With a multitude of data sources in play, transforming raw data into actionable insights is a journey in itself. Advanced analytics incorporate machine learning algorithms and deep learning models to unearth correlations between various factors and predict outcomes. For example, a potential disease outbreak based on specific weather conditions, yield predictions based on soil health, and crop maturity intervals can be ascertained.

Integration of this intelligence into crop management aids in streamlining the farming process. It gives farmers the power to anticipate challenges, strategize solutions ahead of time, and harness optimal conditions for crop growth and productivity.

9.3. Big Data and Precision Agriculture

Precision farming, or precision agriculture, is a methodology that applies technology tools and big data to manage agricultural variation. Though each farm has its unique conditions, big data helps normalize these variations by offering bespoke, field-wise treatment recommendations that streamline cultivation methods and boost productivity.

In-depth insights into soil composition and properties enable farmers to customize seed planting patterns, irrigation schedules, and fertilizer use. Detailed analysis of previous crop yields can forecast future performance and manage agricultural risks effectively. Thus, precision farming empowers farmers to make cultivation more efficient and sustainable.

9.4. Unleashing the Power of Remote Sensing

One of the key sources of big data in agriculture is remote sensing technology. Utilizing drones and satellites, remote sensing captures high-resolution data on soil, crops, and the environment from above — a bird's eye view of the field, if you will.

Most remote sensing devices house multispectral sensors, which mean they register light intensities across various spectral bands, including those beyond human visibility. As plants reflect, absorb, and emit light differently across these bands, these signals provide valuable input about crop health, soil moisture, and potential diseases.

9.5. IoT and Smart Farming

Internet of Things (IoT) technology is another critical element in harnessing big data for crop management. Through IoT devices, farmers can monitor real-time conditions like temperature, humidity, and soil ph levels. They also can track machinery, improve resource allocation, and automate several farming tasks.

Automation and artificial intelligence capabilities mean that these systems don't just collect data; they use it to make decisions autonomously. This could involve dispatching a drone to scan a field for disease or calling in a robot to treat a specific spot with a pest issue.

===Navigating Challenges of Big Data in Agriculture

Despite the myriad opportunities it presents, big data in agriculture is not without its challenges. Data privacy concerns, security risks, lack of skilled personnel, and inequitable access to technology are significant obstacles. Farmers and stakeholders must acknowledge these issues and work towards robust, inclusive solutions to truly harness the transformative potential of big data in crop management.

===Looking Ahead: The Future of Big Data in Crop Management

With an ever-growing acknowledgement of the influence big data holds in crop management and given exponential technological advancements, the future looks promising. Developments like vertical farming, AI-powered decision-making tools, blockchain-powered supply chains, and gene editing, suggest an exciting journey lies ahead.

With the fusion of AI and agronomy, we inch closer to a reality of farms brimming with sensor-laden crops, drones that monitor and treat plant health in real-time, and robotic equipment that performs precise field tasks — a robust, dynamic, and sustainable food production system fueled by big data.

By embracing the big data revolution, we bring about not just a smarter way of managing crops, but a smarter way of managing our planet. Undeniably, this isn't merely about generating elaborate data sets or advanced algorithms; it's about utilizing this intelligence to illuminate our path to a sustainable and food-secure future.

Chapter 10. The Future Plate: How Smart Agriculture Impacts Food Production

In our ever-evolving world, the marriage of technology and agriculture is shaping a futurist vision of farming. The dawn of smart agriculture plays an increasingly pivotal role, not only in the way we cultivate and manage crops but also in our approach to maintaining the food chain.

10.1. Unveiling Smart Agriculture: An Overview

Smart Agriculture is a broad term that encompasses a collection of technologies to help farmers improve productivity and precision in their operations. Using devices and software linked to the Internet of Things (IoT), farmers can monitor crop yields, weather patterns, soil quality, and even livestock health. By efficiently managing resources, Smart Agriculture aids in environmental preservation, financial efficiency, and food security, creating a brilliant solution to confronting the challenges of the burgeoning global population and climate change. It's an approach that earmarks the potential to impact the world's food production significantly.

10.2. Artificial Intelligence in Agriculture

Artificial Intelligence (AI) forms a cornerstone of Smart Agriculture. It enables farmers to analyze and synthesize mountains of data like never before. From predicting optimal planting times using predictive analytics, detecting plant diseases in early stages using image recognition software, to employing GPS-guided autonomous tractors for precise crop management, AI's imprint in agriculture is comprehensive and profoundly transformative.

AI's versatility is further demonstrated with automated robots that help sort and package produce, eliminate weed, or even pick ripe fruits. Computer vision technology enables robots to discern between various stages of a crop lifecycle, allowing precise nurturing of plants, reducing waste, and significantly boosting yield.

10.3. The Automation Revolution

Precision farming depends heavily on automation and it's not difficult to understand why. Automating irrigation systems can ensure the optimum water supply for crops, reducing water wastage, and negating the risk of over or under watering. Additionally, drones equipped with multispectral sensors afford a bird's eye overview of fields, swiftly detecting issues like nutrient deficiencies, pest infestations, or abnormal crop growth patterns. Information thus derived can be used to specifically target problem areas, thus optimizing resource usage and minimizing environmental impact.

Automated data management systems record and analyze patterns related to crop yield, livestock health, and weather that can help farmers make informed decisions. These include what types of crops to plant, the ideal time for cultivation, and the right time for harvest.

10.4. Vertical Farming and Hydroponics

As urbanization expands, Smart Agriculture is venturing beyond traditional farmlands. Vertical farming, a methodology that involves growing crops in vertically stacked layers, is gaining momentum. It leverages LED lights for photosynthesis, requires significantly less water, and maximizes the use of available space, making it a perfect fit for urban environments.

Hydroponics, another avant-garde approach, eliminates the need for soil, substituting it with "nutrient cocktails." When combined with AI's predictive capabilities, both vertical farming and hydroponics ensure constant production, irrespective of weather conditions or seasonal changes.

10.5. AI and Genetically Modified Organisms (GMOs)

Where AI intersects with genetics, it presents a compelling tool for enhancing crop resistance to diseases and pests and adapting to adverse climate changes. By mapping crop genomes and conducting predictive evaluation of genetic modifications, AI can accelerate the development of GMOs. In the long run, it aids in boosting crop yields while preserving biodiversity.

10.6. On the Plate: The Big Picture

The cumulative effects of AI integration in farming ultimately percolate to our plates. Hyperlocal farms could bring fresh produce closer to urban consumers, reducing food miles and nourishing the ideology of farm-to-table gastronomy. Enhanced productivity and decreased costs could pave the way for a more equitable and sustainable food distribution system, bridging the divide between scarcity and abundance.

Smart Agriculture isn't just a collection of futuristic notions. It's a compelling reality defining our present and shaping how we cultivate, manage, distribute, and consume food. As it continues to evolve, we stand on the brink of an agricultural revolution that promises a future where food production is more efficient, profitable, sustainable, and, above all, capable of meeting global food demands.

This future plate, engendered by Smart Agriculture, is not just about nutrition but serves as an emblem of resilience, innovation, and human ingenuity.

Chapter 11. The Road Ahead: Future Potential and Challenges for AI in Agriculture

Heading into the future of agriculture, the use of artificial intelligence (AI) provides an array of promising potentials, presenting a plethora of opportunities yet equally profound challenges. The blend of AI, machine learning, and actionable data can fundamentally transform the traditional farming paradigm, yet several hurdles must be overcome. This dissection of potentiality and barriers seeks to paint an accurate picture of the road ahead.

11.1. The Promise of Precision Agriculture

Fundamentally, AI's greatest potential in agriculture lies in the concept of 'Precision Agriculture.' The continued development of AI tools and techniques can enable farmers to make timely, accurate, and optimized decisions about their farms' management. Precision agriculture focuses on doing exactly what is needed, where and when it's needed on the farm.

For instance, AI-driven drones can collect detailed images of crops, identifying individual plants that may be under stress or diseased. This detailed level of information allows farmers to apply treatments only to specific plants that require attention, rather than treating an entire field, reducing costs and enhancing crop health in a targeted manner. This precise application of resources from fertilizers to water can lead to significant efficiency gains and environmental benefits, potentially revolutionizing farming systems worldwide.

11.2. Harnessing Big Data for Predictive Analytics

A potent aspect of AI in Agriculture is the way it works with Big Data. The proliferation of IoT devices across farming operations inherently produces vast quantities of data. Applying AI to analyze and learn from this data can deliver immense benefits such as predictive analytics. Predictive analytics can aid in the identification of patterns and trends related to factors such as weather, pest activity, crop yield, and soil quality.

The ability of AI to leverage big data for predictive analytics can enable forward-looking decision making. Farmers equipped with these insights can foresee potential problems and implement preemptive solutions, better manage crop rotations and schedules, predict the best times for planting and harvesting, and generally have a better understanding of their operations, optimizing their yields and profits.

11.3. Automated Operations and Robotics

AI brings transformative potential to agriculture through increased automation and introduction of robotics in routine farming operations. Imagine autonomous tractors guided by GPS and AI, field robots programmed to pick ripe crops or robots capable of recognizing weeds and removing them without human intervention.

Automation could raise efficiency while reducing labor needs significantly. Robotic systems integrated with AI could perform intricate tasks with precision day and night, in a wide range of weather conditions, also ensuring human safety by performing potentially dangerous operations.

11.4. Integrating AI with Vertical Farming

Vertical farming is an emerging trend where crops are grown in stacked layers, typically indoors. It allows for the productive use of urban space and offers controlled environments that optimize growth conditions and protect crops from outdoor pests and weather.

AI's integration in such systems could optimize lighting, temperature, humidity, and nutrient delivery tailored to each plant type's specific requirements, automatically adjusting these factors as needed. This level of control and optimization could lead to extraordinarily efficient operations and maximal crop outputs.

11.5. Challenges on the Horizon

Despite these promising possibilities, significant challenges also lie on the road ahead. AI implementation in agriculture requires huge investments in hardware, software, and training, potentially barring small and medium-sized farms.

Limited access to dependable high-speed internet in rural areas often hinders data transfer from farm equipment to AI platforms, preventing real-time analysis. Connectivity is critical for AI's effective deployment and remains a pressing issue for much of our agricultural regions.

Interpreting and acting upon the outputs of AI systems require a degree of technological literacy that may not be present within all farming communities. This digital divide could result in uneven uptake and benefits from AI, with some communities being left behind.

AI's introduction in agriculture might lead to job displacement due to increased automation, raising serious socio-economic issues. These challenges must be addressed through reskilling or upskilling initiatives and appropriate policy frameworks.

Furthermore, with the influx of big data comes the responsibility of data security and privacy. Ensuring this data is used ethically and stored securely will be paramount.

11.6. Conclusion

While AI has the potential to revolutionize agriculture, it is not without its share of challenges. The ability to fully harness its potential will depend on a range of factors including investment, infrastructure, education, and policy support. However, with the global pressures of population growth, changing climates, and the relentless quest for sustainability, it is clear that the road ahead must certainly involve AI as a key driver in the evolution of agriculture. The blend of technology and farming may just be the perfect recipe for feeding the world of tomorrow.

www.ingramcontent.com/pod-product-compliance
Lightning Source LLC
Chambersburg PA
CBHW061054050326
40690CB00012B/2623